Skin Deep

P
Yc
O

CUS

Margaret Hall

www.raintreepublishers.co.uk

Visit our website to find out more information about **Raintree** books.

To order:
☎ Phone 44 (0) 1865 888112
▤ Send a fax to 44 (0) 1865 314091
▢ Visit the Raintree bookshop at **www.raintreepublishers.co.uk** to browse our catalogue and order online.

First published in Great Britain by Raintree,
Halley Court, Jordan Hill, Oxford OX2 8EJ,
part of Harcourt Education.
Raintree is a registered trademark of Harcourt
Education Ltd.

© Harcourt Education Ltd 2007
First published in paperback 2007
The moral right of the proprietor has been asserted.

Editorial: Louise Galpine and Harriet Milles
Design: Michelle Lisseter and Bigtop
Illustrations: Darren Lingard
Picture Research: Mica Brancic and Maria Joannou
Production: Camilla Crask

Originated by Modern Age
Printed and bound in China by WKT Company
Limited

10-digit ISBN 1 406 20473 0 (hardback)
13-digit ISBN 978 1 4062 0473 5
11 10 09 08 07
10 9 8 7 6 5 4 3 2 1

10-digit ISBN 1 406 20498 6 (paperback)
13-digit ISBN 978-1-4062-0498-8
11 10 09 08 07
10 9 8 7 6 5 4 3 2 1

**British Library
Cataloguing in Publication Data**
Hall, Margaret
Skin deep. - (Fusion): Functions of skin
612.7'9
A full catalogue record for this book is available from
the British Library.

Acknowledgements
The publishers would like to thank the following for
permission to reproduce photographs: Alamy **pp**. 20
(Applestock), **19** (Stock Connection Distribution);
Corbis **pp. 5** (Zefa/A Moller), **13** (Joe McBride), **21**
(Claire Artman), **25** (Ruediger Knobloch/A.B./Zefa),
28 (Alfred Saerchinger/Zefa), **7** (Robert Essel); Getty
Images **pp. 11** (Stone), **17** (Barbara Peacock), **27**
(The Image Bank), **29** (Photodisc); Harcourt
Education **p. 16**; Rex Features/Image Source **p. 29**;
Science Picture Library **pp. 9** (Jane Shemilt), **23**
(Eye of Science), **15** (Biophoto Associates).

Cover photograph of a scanning electron micrograph
(SEM) of the surface of human skin, reproduced with
permission of Science Photo Library (CNRI).

Every effort has been made to contact copyright
holders of any material reproduced in this book. Any
omissions will be rectified in subsequent printings if
notice is given to the publishers.

The publishers would like to thank Nancy Harris and
Harold Pratt for their assistance with the preparation
of this book.

Disclaimer
All the Internet addresses (URLs) given in this book
were valid at the time of going to press. However, due
to the dynamic nature of the Internet, some
addresses may have changed, or sites may have
changed or ceased to exist since publication. While
the author and publishers regret any inconvenience
this may cause readers, no responsibility for any
such changes can be accepted by either the author
or the publishers.

It is recommended that adults supervise children on
the Internet.

Contents

Some words are printed in bold, **like this**. You can find out what they mean on page 30. You can also look in the box at the bottom of the page where they first appear.

The skin you're in: reasons to respect it

You probably do not think too much about your skin. But maybe you should. After all, skin is pretty amazing!

Skin is an **organ**. Organs are parts of the body that do a certain job. Skin is your body's largest organ. It covers you from your head to your feet.

Like all organs, skin does important work. It protects your whole body. It helps control your temperature. It helps you feel and move. These are just some of the jobs skin does. There are many reasons to be happy with the skin you are in.

Different skin

Animals' bodies are covered with skin, too. But animal skin is often very different from your skin. An elephant's skin is thick and wrinkled. It is ten times thicker than the skin on your body!

organ   part of the body that does a certain job

5

▲ *Your whole body*
is covered with
a layer of skin.

It's alive!

Your skin is a living thing. All living things are made of **cells**. Cells are like tiny building blocks.

Your skin has two layers. The layer you can see is the **epidermis**. It is thinner than a sheet of paper. The epidermis is made of old skin cells.

This drawing shows what ▼ the layers of your skin look like. The layers are much thicker in the drawing than they are on your body.

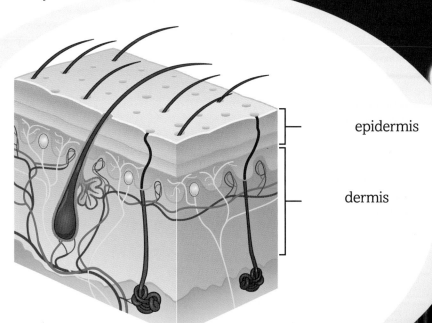

epidermis

dermis

cell	tiny building block that makes up different parts of the body
dermis	lower layer of skin
epidermis	top layer of skin

The layer beneath the epidermis is called the **dermis**. New skin cells grow in this layer. These cells move up towards the epidermis. Old skin cells flake off. Then new cells take their place. This keeps happening again and again.

New skin!

Take a good look at your skin. In about a month, all the skin you see will be gone. Your body will have made a whole new layer of skin!

It's tough

Your skin is tough. It protects your bones. It also protects your muscles. It protects other **organs** such as your heart and lungs.

Under your skin is a layer of fat. Your body needs this fat. It acts like padding. It protects you when you bump into something. It protects you when something bumps into you.

Skin keeps **germs** outside your body. Germs are tiny living things. They are found everywhere. Germs are on books, and even in the air. If germs get inside your body, they can make you sick.

Germs can get into your body through a cut. A cut is an open place in the skin. It is important to wash a cut. Then put a germ-killing medicine on it.

blood vessel   tiny tube that carries blood through the body
germ   tiny living thing that can cause sickness

Bumps and bruises

*If you bump yourself hard, your skin will bruise. Tiny **blood vessels** in the skin will break. Blood vessels are tiny tubes that carry blood through the body. The dark patch you see is blood under the skin.*

▼ *Germs could get inside your body through a cut like this.*

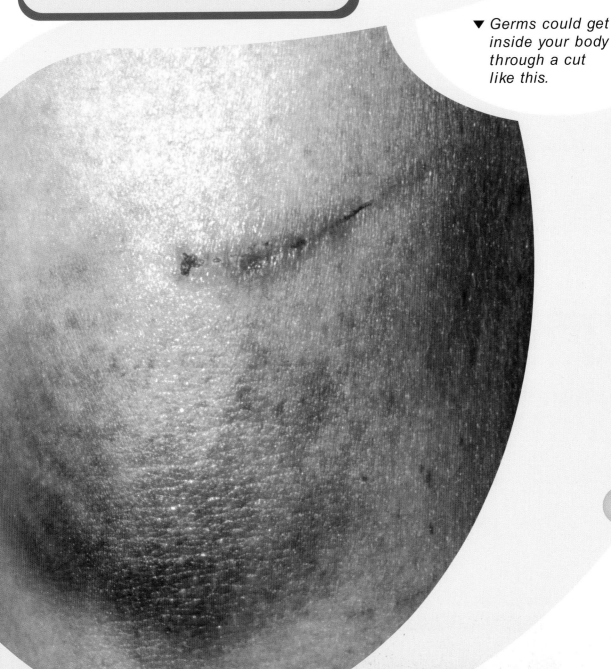

It's waterproof

Without skin, your body would be like a big sponge. When you got wet your body would soak up water.

Luckily your skin is like a big raincoat. It keeps your insides from getting wet. Water cannot get through your skin when you swim or take a bath.

A thin layer of **oil** makes your body waterproof. Oil is a slippery liquid. This oil is made in the **dermis**. The dermis is the lower layer of skin. The oil rises to the top of your skin.

When you touch things, oil from your fingers stays behind. That is how you leave fingerprints.

Water wrinkles

Does your skin wrinkle after a long bath? If you spend a long time in the water, oil washes off your skin. Then, a little water can get into the top layer of skin. No one knows why this makes skin wrinkle. It might be because the water stretches the skin.

10

oil   slippery liquid that does not dissolve in (become part of) water

▲ Water slides right off your skin.

It's your body's air conditioner

Your skin is your body's air conditioner. Sometimes your body gets too hot. Then, your skin helps make heat leave your body. Some heat leaves your skin through tiny openings. These openings are called **pores**.

Trapping heat

Your skin also helps keep you warm. When you get cold, hairs on your skin stand up straight. This helps the hairs trap heat. The hairs keep heat close to your skin. Goosebumps form on the skin where the hairs stand up.

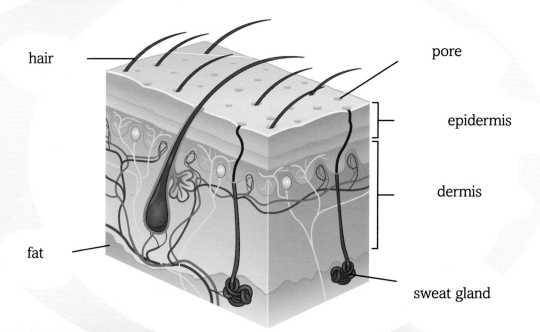

hair

pore

epidermis

dermis

fat

sweat gland

12

pore	very small opening in the skin
sweat	salty water that leaves the body through the skin
sweat gland	part of the skin where sweat is made

Salty water called **sweat** also goes out of pores. When you get hot, parts of your skin sweat. These parts are called **sweat glands**. The sweat moves to the top layer of your skin. It comes out of the pores. Then it dries. This cools off your skin.

Sweating helps your body get rid of things it does not need. These things are called waste.

A hard game of ▶ tennis makes you hot. Sweating cools you down.

It makes a vitamin

Your skin uses sunlight to make an important vitamin. This is **vitamin D**. It is sometimes called the "sunshine vitamin". You need this vitamin to help your bones grow strong. You need vitamin D to keep your teeth strong and healthy.

Some of the vitamin D you need comes from food. But most of this vitamin comes from the Sun. Your skin makes vitamin D from special rays in sunlight. You need to spend at least 30 minutes in the Sun every week to make enough vitamin D.

Not enough vitamin D can sometimes cause problems. It can make bones soft and weak. The bones of very young children can grow bent. Luckily not many people have these problems. They can get better with medicine.

vitamin D   something that helps bones grow and stay strong

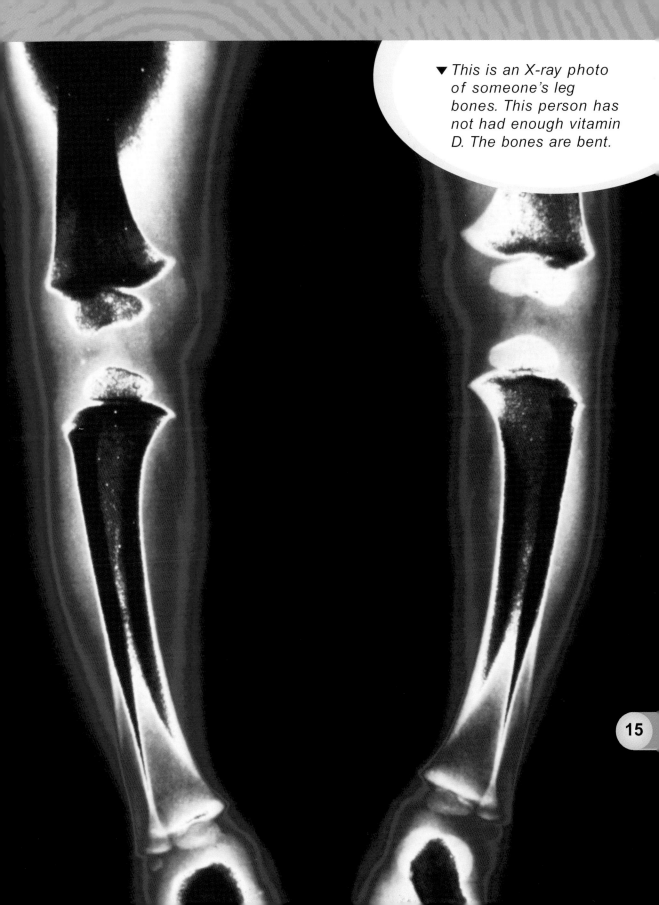

▼ This is an X-ray photo of someone's leg bones. This person has not had enough vitamin D. The bones are bent.

15

It has colour

Stand in front of a mirror with a friend. Is your skin exactly the same colour as your friend's? It is probably at least a little different. Everyone's skin has a brown colouring. This colouring is called **melanin**. The more melanin your skin has, the darker it is.

Your skin colour ▼ depends on how much melanin your skin makes.

melanin	part of the skin that produces colour
sunscreen	cream that keeps some rays from the Sun from harming your skin

Melanin helps protect skin from the Sun. When people go in the sun, their bodies make more melanin. Their skin slowly darkens. They get a suntan.

People with dark skin already have a lot of melanin. It is already protecting their skin. But too much hot sunshine is dangerous for anyone. It can burn the skin.

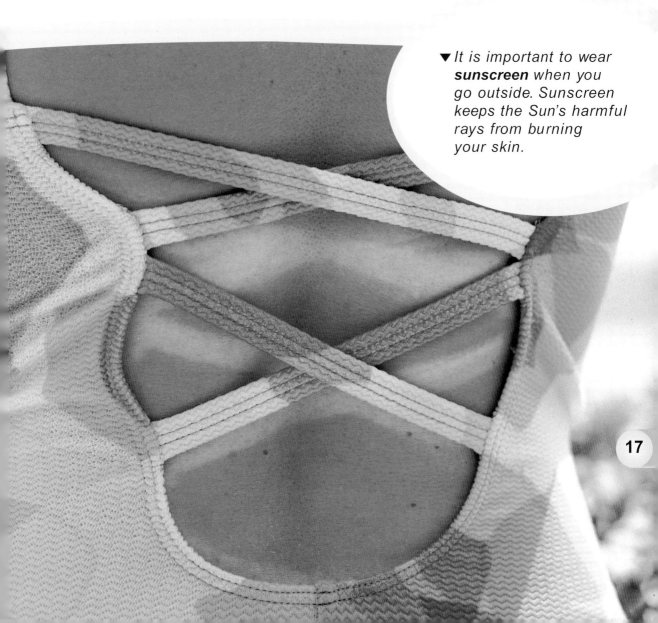

▼ It is important to wear **sunscreen** when you go outside. Sunscreen keeps the Sun's harmful rays from burning your skin.

It can feel

What if you did not have a sense of touch? You could get burned when you grab something hot. You could freeze your fingers on something cold.

Your skin is important for your sense of touch. The surface of your skin has millions of **nerve endings**. These are special **cells**. They carry messages between your skin and your brain.

What happens if you touch something sharp or hot? Your nerve endings send a warning. The warning tells the muscles in your hand to pull away. This happens so fast that you do not even think about it.

Nerve endings in your skin also let your brain know if things are cold. They let you know if things are dry, soft, or hard.

Nerve endings

Your whole body is covered with nerve endings. Your fingers, toes, lips, and tongue have the most nerve endings. The middle of your back has the least.

nerve endings special cells that carry messages between the skin and the brain

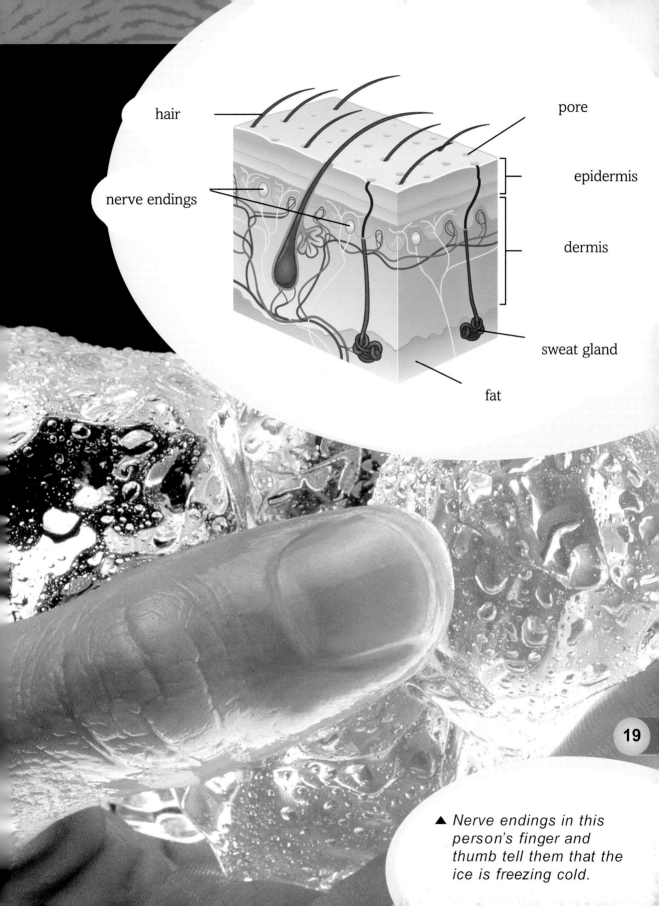

hair

pore

epidermis

nerve endings

dermis

sweat gland

fat

▲ *Nerve endings in this person's finger and thumb tell them that the ice is freezing cold.*

It's stretchy

Stretch your arms up over your head. Now, twist at the waist. What does your skin do? It stretches and twists along with you!

Skin gets its stretch from something called **elastin**. Elastin is found in the **dermis**. The dermis is the lower layer of skin.

No matter how ▶
you move, your
skin moves and
stretches with you.

20

elastin something that makes skin stretchy

As people get older, their skin gets thinner. The skin also loses some elastin. So, an old person's skin is not as stretchy as a young person's skin.

When you get old, your skin might look wrinkled. This is partly because your skin has less elastin. It is also because older skin has less water. Water in the skin helps skin stay smooth.

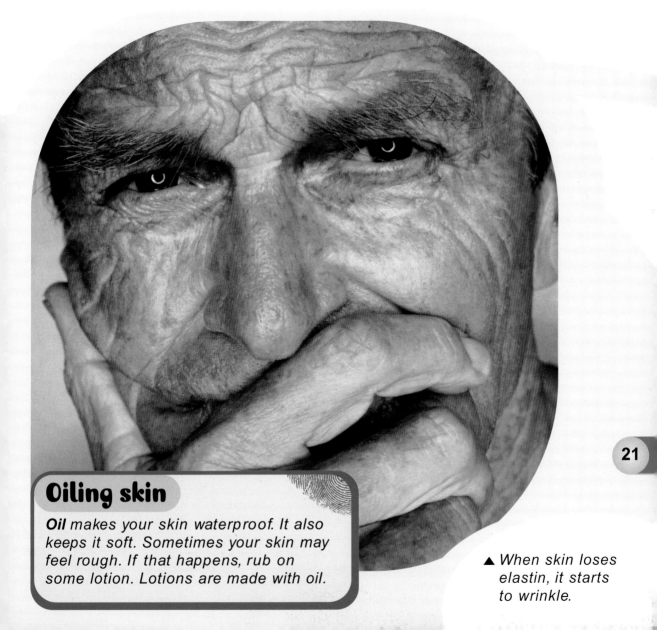

Oiling skin

Oil makes your skin waterproof. It also keeps it soft. Sometimes your skin may feel rough. If that happens, rub on some lotion. Lotions are made with oil.

▲ When skin loses elastin, it starts to wrinkle.

It heals itself

Your skin is tough. However, it can be hurt.

Small cuts and scrapes do not bleed. That is because no **blood vessels** (tiny tubes) carry blood to the top layer of skin. There are blood vessels in the lower layer. So, a deep cut or scrape will bleed.

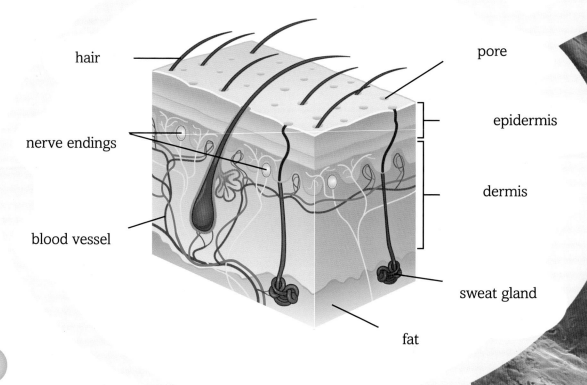

hair

nerve endings

blood vessel

pore

epidermis

dermis

sweat gland

fat

scab   thick, tough patch of skin that grows to protect a cut or scrape

Your body works to heal cuts on its own. Special **cells** (tiny building blocks) in the blood hurry to the cut. They make a thick, tough covering called a **scab**.

A scab protects hurt skin. It keeps **germs** out. It stops germs causing sickness. New skin starts to grow under the scab. When the new skin is fully grown, the scab falls off.

▼ *In this microscope picture, blood is forming into a scab on cut skin.*

It's more than a body covering

Take a good look at your arm and hand. Your hair and fingernails are a lot like skin.

New skin **cells** move up to the surface of the skin. Most of these new cells take the place of old skin cells. But some change into flat, hard cells. They are called **keratin**. These cells become hair, fingernails, and toenails.

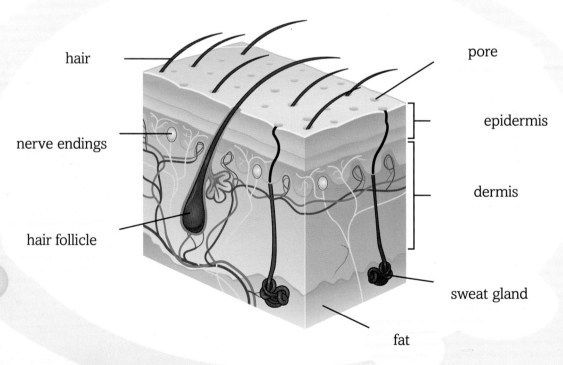

hair

nerve endings

hair follicle

pore

epidermis

dermis

sweat gland

fat

24

hair follicle	tiny tube from which a hair grows
keratin	substance made of flat, hard skin cells

Most of your body is covered with hair. Hair starts to grow in the **dermis**. The dermis is the second layer of skin. Every hair on your body grows in its own little tube. These tubes are called **hair follicles**.

The cells that form your fingernails start under the skin. So do the cells that form your toenails. Your hair and nails are always growing. The parts you can see are made of old, dead cells. That is why it does not hurt to cut them.

▼ The keratin cells that make nails and hair were formed in your skin.

Take care of your skin

Your skin is important. You need to take good care of it. Here are a few tips for keeping your skin healthy:

- Keep it clean. Use water and mild soap to wash your skin.

- Drink lots of water. This keeps your skin soft and smooth.

- Take care of cuts and scrapes. Wash a small cut or scrape. Cover it with a bandage to keep out dirt and **germs**. Ask an adult to help you take care of big cuts.

- Try to stay out of the Sun at midday. That is when the Sun's harmful rays are the strongest.

- Use **sunscreen** whenever you go out in the Sun.

UV Index Number	Description	Advice
1–2	Low danger of damage from the Sun.	People with very light skin should wear sunscreen.
3–5	Some danger of damage from the Sun.	Wear clothing that covers the skin. Stay in the shade during the middle of the day.
6–7	High danger of damage from the Sun.	Stay out of the Sun between 10 a.m. and 4 p.m. Wear a hat and sunglasses. Use sunscreen.
8–10	Very high danger of damage from the Sun.	Stay out of the Sun as much as possible. Wear a hat and sunglasses. Use sunscreen and put it on often.

This chart is called the UV Index. ▲ It helps people know how much danger there is from the Sun. Many weather reports give a UV Index number.

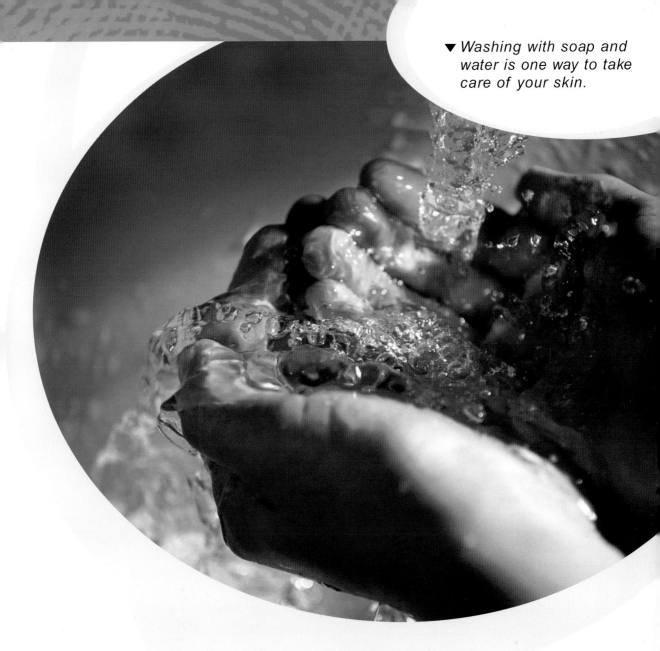

▼ *Washing with soap and water is one way to take care of your skin.*

Protection

Sunscreen is labelled with numbers called SPF numbers. SPF means "Sun Protection Factor". Use a sunscreen that is SPF 15 or higher. Higher numbers mean more protection from the Sun.

Skin fun and facts!

Now you know how amazing your skin really is. It is one of your body's most important **organs**. Always look after your skin, and treat it with respect!

Imagine that you could take off ▶ your skin and flatten it. It would be about the size of a beach towel. An adult's skin would be the size of a double-bed sheet.

◀ Skin is the heaviest part of your body. An adult's skin weighs about 11 kilograms (24 pounds).

Your skin is thickest on the ▲ bottom of your feet. If you go barefoot a lot, this skin gets even thicker.

▼ A peacock's feathers are like your hair and nails. They are also made from **keratin**. Keratin is a substance made of flat, hard skin **cells**. A horse's hooves are made of keratin. So are a porcupine's quills, and a cow's horns.

29

Glossary

blood vessel tiny tube that carries blood through the body

cell tiny building block that makes up different parts of the body. Skin is made up of millions of cells.

dermis lower layer of skin. The dermis is thicker than the epidermis.

elastin something that makes skin stretchy. Without elastin, your skin could not bend.

epidermis top layer of skin. The epidermis is the part of your skin that you see.

germ tiny living thing that can cause sickness. Germs cause sickness when they get inside your body.

hair follicle tiny tube from which a hair grows. Every hair on your body has its own hair follicle.

keratin substance made of flat, hard skin cells. It forms hair, fingernails, and toenails.

melanin part of the skin that produces colour. The more melanin a person has, the darker his or her skin is.

nerve endings special cells that carry messages between the skin and the brain. There are millions of nerve endings in your skin.

oil slippery liquid that does not dissolve in (become part of) water

organ part of the body that does a certain job. The heart, lungs, brain, and skin are all organs.

pore very small opening in the skin. Sweat escapes from your body through pores.

scab thick, tough patch of skin that grows to protect a cut or scrape. A scab falls off when new skin grows.

sunscreen cream that keeps some rays from the Sun from harming your skin. Without sunscreen, you can get sunburned.

sweat salty water that leaves the body through the skin. Sweat is a waste product made by your body.

sweat gland part of the skin where sweat is made. Sweat glands are found in the dermis.

vitamin D something that helps bones grow and stay strong. Your body gets most of the vitamin D it needs from sunshine.

Want to know more?

Books to read

- *Microlife That Makes Us Ill*, Steve Parker (Raintree, 2005)
- *My Amazing Body: Senses*, Angela Royston (Raintree, 2004)
- *Why Do I Get a Sunburn?: And Other Questions About Skin,* Angela Royston (Heinemann Library, 2003)

Websites

- http://www.kidshealth.org/kid/body/skin_noSW.html
  Learn all about your body's largest organ.
- http://yucky.kids.discovery.com/noflash/body/pg000146.html
  Find out about the many jobs skin does.

Read about the amazing way that your body fights diseases in ***Body Warriors***.

See what other parts of your body can do when they are all working well in ***Are You Tough Enough***?

Index